MALCOLM H

MEDIEVAL MASONS

SHIRE ARCHAEOLOGY

Cover illustrations:
(Left) Rubble walling at Bolton Castle, Wensleydale, North Yorkshire.
(Upper right) A fourteenth-century stained glass panel from the church of St Mary
Magdalene at Helmdon, Northamptonshire, depicting a mason, William Campion, wielding
his mason's axe (by courtesy of the Reverend J. H. Roberts, Helmdon Church).
(Lower right) A mason's mark at Warkworth Castle, Northumberland.

British Library Cataloguing in Publication Data:
Hislop, Malcolm
Medieval masons. – (Shire archaeology; 78)
1. Masonry – Great Britain – History
2. Architecture, Medieval – Great Britain
3. Excavations (Archaeology) – Great Britain
I. Title 693.1'0941'0902
ISBN 0 7478 0461 3

Published in 2000 by
SHIRE PUBLICATIONS LTD
Cromwell House, Church Street, Princes Risborough,
Buckinghamshire HP27 9AA, UK.
(Website: www.shirebooks.co.uk)

Series Editor: James Dyer.

Number 78 in the Shire Archaeology series.

ISBN 0 7478 0461 3.

First published 2000.

Printed in Great Britain by
CIT Printing Services Ltd, Press Buildings,
Merlins Bridge, Haverfordwest, Pembrokeshire SA61 1XF.

Contents

Acknowledgements

Quotations from the chronicles concerning Abingdon, Beverley, Canterbury, Gloucester, Ramsey and St Albans are taken from translations in L. F. Salzman, *Building in England Down to 1540* (Oxford University Press, 1952). Those from the building accounts of Dover Castle, Westminster Abbey and Palace, and Winchester Castle are from H. M. Colvin and L. C. Hector (editors), *Building Accounts of Henry III* (Oxford University Press, 1972).

English Heritage and the Dean and Chapter of Peterborough Cathedral are owed thanks for their respective permissions to examine and photograph the inner ditch of Beeston Castle and the windlass in the north-west tower of Peterborough Cathedral.

Thanks for permission to use illustrations are due to the British Library, Dr Richard Fawcett and the Norfolk and Norwich Archaeological Society, the Ministry of Defence, the Public Record Office, the Reverend J. H. Roberts, the University of Cambridge Museum of Archaeology and Anthropology and Dr Christopher Wilson.

Dr Richard Fawcett was kind enough to read a draft of this book and to make several suggestions for its improvement. However, the author is fully responsible for the views expressed and the accuracy of the information imparted in the published text.

List of illustrations

1
Introduction

Today, when masoncraft is little more than a specialist sideline of construction, making little or no impact on the main thrust of architectural development, it is not always easy to recapture its erstwhile importance. For in the Middle Ages stone was the pre-eminent building material for most major works of architecture, and consequently masons were usually the senior partners in the alliance of craftsmanship that existed during an important building project.

The master mason encompassed the functions of both architect and builder, two occupations that have long since been separated. A modern student of the subject may therefore see a dichotomy at the heart of medieval masoncraft in that it contains both intellectual and pragmatic dimensions. Predictably, perhaps, scholarship has tended to concern itself with the intellectual rather than with the pragmatic. The principal concern has been with the master mason in his artistic capacity, as the progenitor of an individual style, and less emphasis has been placed on the structural aspects of his work. However, the key to understanding the practice of architecture in the Middle Ages is to recognise that, although aesthetics were undoubtedly part of the master mason's brief, he was first and foremost an engineer, concerned with the practicalities of construction.

The freemasons were the elite: they cut and dressed the good-quality freestone that was used for carved work, quoins and ashlar blocks, and were regarded as the most skilful amongst the various categories of masons, a status that is reflected in their higher wages. It is generally assumed that the masons who functioned as architects were drawn from the freemasons' ranks. Some undoubtedly were, but it is worth remembering that, although the freemason had to understand the significance of the sometimes elaborately shaped stones that he worked on, he was generally confined to his lodge and divorced from the main construction process. It is therefore arguable that the mason layers, who placed the stones into position, and the rough masons, who built rubble walling, were in a better position to comprehend the structural implications of building. The mason's craft encompassed a range of skills and specialities and, whatever the background of the architect, he was able to draw upon the expertise of others. Leadership and organisational abilities were more important attributes than particular craft skills.

Much of our knowledge about the medieval mason and his craft is owed to the fortunate survival in England of a substantial body of documentary evidence. These written records have formed the backbone of attempts to elucidate the nature of building during the Middle Ages. Whilst they provide some fascinating insights into the subject, a study based wholly on the written evidence has its drawbacks because medieval terminology can be ambiguous, and the documents themselves are limited in what they can tell us about the essentials of design and construction.

This book lays greater emphasis than has been usual on the evidence to be gleaned from archaeological excavation and survey, and draws attention to what an examination of the surviving medieval buildings can reveal about the subject. Except in the field of stylistic development, where they have played an indispensable part, the buildings themselves are probably an under-used resource. The archaeological study of buildings can nevertheless provide us with a good deal of extra information about the practice of masoncraft. It can confirm, contradict or elaborate upon documented methods, and suggest answers to some of the questions posed by the written sources.

To take an example, documents may tell us something about the sources of building stone, but it is the excavation of quarry sites that will provide more detailed information about extraction methods. Similarly, written records might indicate the purchase of scaffolding materials but it is only archaeological investigation that will reveal how they were employed on a particular site. A greater stumbling-block to our understanding of masonic methods is that for the majority of sites documentary sources are limited or non-existent. In these instances archaeology will be the most important or only source of information available to us. Only when more excavation work and survey work has been done will we be in a position to present a more comprehensive view of medieval masoncraft and be able to expound more fully on chronological and regional differences in techniques.

Potentially, one of the most interesting aspects of research into medieval masoncraft is the reconstruction of the careers of individual mason architects and the identification of the distinguishing features of their work. The documentary spadework has been done, and a number of interesting architectural studies have been completed, but there is still work to be undertaken in the field of buildings archaeology before we will be able to comprehend fully the process of building design and construction and the master mason's role in it. Some of the difficulties presented by the subject are summarised in the final chapter of this volume.

Suffice it to say for the moment that the essence of the mason architect is to be found in his craft-based training and his empirical approach to design and construction, whereby theory and practice were sometimes formulated in tandem. There was no universal technical manual, and challenges of structure and design were anticipated only in the light of past experience. In these circumstances there could be no substitute for the presence of the master mason on the building site, directing operations and solving problems as they presented themselves. It is to be hoped that this book will give insights into the practical world of the medieval mason and his craft, and that it will engender greater interest in, and encourage further research into, a subject about which the definitive work has yet to be written.

2
Documentary evidence

Documentary evidence for medieval masons and the manner in which they worked falls into three main categories. These are: chronicles; administrative documents, of which building accounts and contracts are the most important; and what I have termed 'masonic manuscripts', a miscellany of manuals, notebooks, statutes and ordinances in which some of the traditions and practices of the trade are recorded.

Chronicles

Virtually the only documentary sources for the earliest part of the Middle Ages are the chronicles of certain religious houses. There is very little technical information in them and their main usefulness is for the architectural history of the houses concerned. However, they occasionally provide us with the names of the principal craftsmen and give insights into working practices and the sequence of construction. The most valuable is that of Gervase of Canterbury, who wrote a vivid account of the fire that severely damaged the cathedral choir in 1174 and of the subsequent reconstruction of the building. Gervase conveys an impression of the range of accomplishments that the master mason of a major building project might be expected to have. The man appointed by the authorities was one William of Sens, 'a craftsman most skilful in both wood and stone', who was retained 'on account of his lively genius and good reputation'. His 'lively genius' suggests an inventiveness above and beyond that which might have been expected of the average working mason and, indeed, the master mason of an important project had to be a man of many parts.

His architectural role encompassed both planning and details: William of Sens designed the templates that acted as patterns for the stone-cutters when shaping moulded stones. In addition, he had to mastermind the logistics of obtaining and transporting the building materials (in the case of Canterbury the stone was brought 'from beyond the sea', probably from the quarries of Caen in Normandy), and was responsible for constructing machinery to be used in the work; in the words of Gervase, William of Sens 'constructed ingenious machines for loading and unloading ships and for lifting masonry and stones'.

Not all craftsmen could emulate the broader role that was expected of a competent master. The experience of St Albans Abbey contrasts markedly with that of Canterbury. Despite being a 'craftsman of great reputation', Master Hugh de Goldclif, who was appointed to rebuild the abbey church during the time of Abbot John (1195–1214), is described elsewhere in the chronicle as 'a deceitful and unreliable man'. Whether this is an accurate evaluation, or whether the mason was a useful scapegoat or simply an incompetent manager, it certainly appears that the project was beset with problems. The work progressed tediously slowly, and the walls were left uncovered during the 'rainy season', causing the stone to break up and the new work to collapse.

Both Canterbury and St Albans provide glimpses of the interaction between the master craftsman and the patron. As the acknowledged technical authority, the master mason could have great influence on the scale and character of the work. The patron was, to a degree, in thrall to his expert opinion and persuasive powers. It was only when the monks of Canterbury had become somewhat comforted with the thought that works were in hand to repair the fire-damaged choir that William of Sens broke the news that complete reconstruction was the only feasible option. It was the approach of a diplomat; such inter-personal accomplishments were a useful adjunct to technical mastery. Whilst such specialist skill may have been held in great respect, the 'mystery' of masoncraft could also be held in suspicion. The St Albans chronicler is scathing about the 'carved work, unnecessary, trifling, and beyond measure costly' which was added 'by the treacherous advice' of Master Hugh de Goldclif.

The contrasting attitudes towards masters William and Hugh reveal a little of the inconsistent results of medieval building; it could be something of a lottery, especially in the early period before the technical achievements of the Gothic had placed the craft on a more consistent footing. The chronicles highlight the empiric nature of masoncraft in the early Middle Ages, and its generally unscientific approach to construction. There are numerous accounts of structural failure. Around 985 a crack opened up in 'the higher tower' of Ramsey Abbey church, a disaster that was attributed to the 'lack of foresight of the masons'. In 1091 the tower of Abingdon Abbey fell down, perhaps disturbed by the recent demolition of adjacent works, and about 1170 the west tower of Gloucester Abbey church collapsed 'through a defect in the foundations'. Around 1200 it was decided to raise a spire on top of the eleventh-century central tower of Beverley Minster; its subsequent fall was again attributed to the masons. As the chronicler relates, the masons in charge 'were not as cautious as was necessary, not as prudent as they were cunning in their craft; they were concerned rather with beauty than with strength, rather with effect than with the need for safety'. The vision of the artist was not always mitigated by the pragmatism of the engineer.

Building accounts

Towards the middle of the thirteenth century detailed accounts start to appear for individual building projects undertaken by the Crown.

Essentially lists of wages paid, purchases made and summaries of expenditure incurred, the royal accounts, together with the series of warrants that preceded and accompanied a great building project, form an important body of reference for the student of architectural history. These royal accounts are supplemented by those from a number of religious houses. In addition a few survive from the secular nobility, the most important being those of the Duchy of Lancaster.

Building accounts are invaluable for estimating the cost of a project and, because they are arranged systematically, according to date, for tracing the chronological and sequential development of a building. It has to be said that they are less useful in respect of technical details, but occasionally they throw sidelights on the process of construction. An entry in the Winchester Castle accounts, for example, refers to the making of fifty iron clamps 'to bind the tower', thereby drawing attention to the use of metal reinforcement in medieval masonry work. Amongst the final payments for the Westminster Palace account of 1259 is one for two hundredweight of reeds to cover a wall; another is for straw for the same wall. These items, appearing as they do at the end of the building season, signify the practice of covering up unfinished masonry to protect it against water penetration and frost damage.

Another process that the accounts help to illuminate is the supply and preparation of lime mortar. It is clear that in some instances lime was burnt on site. The accounts for Winchester Castle record a payment to 'Adam the lime-man for making one kiln', and there is more than one reference to 'wood to fire the kiln'. In other cases lime was purchased from specialist lime-burners, and, although their location is seldom mentioned, payments for transportation to the building site show that they were not based in the immediate vicinity of the works. Some of these specialists were mentioned by name: Bartholomew, who supplied Dover Castle in the 1220s, and Richard and Agnes, from whom purchases were made for Westminster Abbey in the 1250s. In addition there are numerous payments recorded for slaking lime. Confirmation that this process was carried out on site comes from the Dover Castle accounts of 1227, where a payment is recorded for the 'portage of 1120 loads of water to the ditches and to slake the lime there'.

Regarding the materials, many of the entries are simply records of items bought, but sometimes the function of particular purchases was specified, as in the case of scaffolding and centring. The Westminster Abbey accounts, for instance, record that in 1253 willow and alder, withies and hurdles were bought 'for scaffolding', whereas the accounts for Winchester Castle demonstrate that withies and poles were bought for the same purpose in 1258. Details of wages paid specifically to scaffold erectors suggest that in some cases the construction of scaffolding was considered a specialist task. Materials for the construction of centring are frequently mentioned. At Dover, for example, three hundred boards of beech were acquired for 'centers' and one hundred laths 'to make centring'. At Winchester Castle in 1258, thirty-eight boards were bought 'to make centring'. The reference in the same account to nails for centring reminds us of the temporary nature of such structures.

Of particular interest is the information the accounts provide about the supply and working of stone. The masonry for the works of the 1220s at Winchester Castle came from quarries at Selborne in Hampshire, Haslebury in Somerset, the Isle of Wight and Caen in Normandy. The nature of some of the payments suggests that the stone was extracted in blocks of specified size. Thus in July 1222 Richard the quarryman of Selborne received £2 0s 0d for one thousand stones to be taken out of his quarry, and in August Richard Sired was paid £1 3s 4d to break up and extract 105 stones from Haslebury quarry.

The Isle of Wight appears to have been the source of much of the good-quality stone. In July 1222 two individuals, Payn of Christchurch and Morand, each supplied the works with 1000 feet (304.8 metres) of Isle of Wight stone. The specified length hints at regularly shaped masonry, and indeed other entries concerning these two suppliers are

1. The building contract of 1378 for Roxburgh Castle. (Public Record Office)

unambiguous in referring to dressed stone. In November, for instance, Payn supplied the works with 1757 'coins and ashlars' and Morand supplied '500 Isle of Wight stones, that is coins and ashlars'. Entries like these demonstrate that stone was sometimes obtained from contractors ready dressed, but others demonstrate the opposite. The payment in the Westminster Palace accounts of 1259 for carrying worked stones from the masons' lodge to the king's chamber, where it was to be used for the chimney, shows fairly conclusively that the stone was worked on site.

Most workers appear to have been paid a day rate in the thirteenth century, though some work was carried out 'at task', whereby the mason agreed to carry out a job for a fixed fee or piecework rate. Thus in 1253 'Bernard & Reginald with their fellows' were paid 'for 2504 feet [763.2 metres] of ashlar cut at task' for Westminster Abbey. Task work contracts were not confined to cutting quantities of dressed stone: at Dover in 1221 Richard Norris was paid for making two foundations for the new gate, and in 1259 at Westminster Palace 3s 6d was paid out for making $4^1/2$ perches of a wall by task. Contracts may have been drawn up in connection with these tasks, but if so they have not survived and the laconic entries in the building accounts are all the evidence that remains.

Building contracts

Masonic building contracts are extant from *c*.1300 onwards (figure 1). They were drawn up as indentures, that is to say, they were duplicated on a single sheet (usually parchment) and the copies divided from one another along an indented line. Each copy was endorsed with the seal of one of the contracting parties (figure 2). It should be remembered that their main purpose was to describe the respective responsibilities of the patron and building contractor. Most important are the rates and terms of payment and what the contractor was expected to do and provide in return for his money. The contents of these documents, therefore, support this principal aim, and information about masonic practice tends to be incidental. For example, whilst there may be many references to the reuse of old materials, this is because recycling had an economic advantage; technical detail, however, is lacking.

Descriptions of the buildings to be erected range from Master John of Burcestre's vague brief of 1348 to 'build a castle on the motte' of Stafford, to quite detailed specifications that include measurements. Interestingly, even where the descriptions are specific they do not always correspond with the surviving buildings themselves. For example, a comparison of the building contract of 1378 for part of Bolton Castle in North Yorkshire and the completed buildings highlights important disparities. Such anomalies sometimes result from changes of plan,

2. The seal of the fourteenth-century master mason Thomas Crump. In the centre is a capital T and around the border the name CRVMP. (By permission of the British Library)

most likely at the instigation of the patron. In other instances it might be the oversight or fraudulent practice of the mason that is to blame. It is recorded in an indenture of 1381, for instance, that Thomas Crump, in building the great gatehouse of Cooling (or Cowling) Castle in Kent, had not made a postern as he had agreed to do. He had also overcharged his client, Sir John Cobham, by 100 shillings by accounting for 2^1/$_2$ perches more than he had built. The 'cowboy' builder is by no means a modern phenomenon.

A few of the indentures provide evidence that masons sometimes failed to complete buildings. When Henry Middleton undertook to reconstruct the dormitory of Durham Priory in 1398, the written agreement provided for exactly this eventuality. By spelling out that the prior would only be bound to pay for work completed, and that the mason and four others would be held in a bond of £40 each to match the periodic payments to be made to the mason, the risk to the priory was minimised. These were wise precautions, because Henry Middleton evidently did not fulfil his obligations and the dormitory had to be completed under a second contract of 1401–2 by a different mason.

Contracts sometimes touch on the responsibility for design. The indenture of 1359 for the eastern chapels of Vale Royal Abbey, Cheshire, includes the clause that the master mason, William de Helpeston, should have control over the design of the mouldings and that he should be allowed to alter them at will. That it was felt necessary to insert such a stipulation may suggest that it was not always the practice to allow a mason such freedom and that in some other cases the patron may have reserved the right of approval.

This example is particularly apposite given that some contracting masons were apparently working to the designs of another party. It is made clear in the contract of 1315 for the construction of a perimeter wall around Eltham manor house in south-east London that the four contractors were to be guided by the advice of the royal mason, Master Michael of Canterbury. Similarly, in 1395 Richard Washbrook and John Swallow undertook to make a cornice for the head of the wall of Westminster Palace Hall 'according to the purport of a form and mould made by the counsel of Master Henry Yevele'. This is one of three late fourteenth-century contracts with masons in which Henry Yevele, the famous master mason, features in a capacity other than that of contractor. When Nicholas Typerton undertook to construct the foundations of the south aisle and porch of St Dunstan's church in London he was to make them 'according to the scheme of Henry Yevele'. This appears to be another case in which Yevele provided a design and another mason the labour, but his role is less clear in the case of Cooling Castle, where an endorsement to the contract records that Thomas Crump's overcharging came to light through an audit made by Yevele.

There are a few instances in which the contracting mason is referred to one or more models for the design of the building in hand. The stonework of the new dormitory of Durham Priory, for instance, was to be like that of the Constable Tower of Brancepeth Castle; the chapel that the mason Thomas Betes agreed to build in 1433 for the church of St Mary-on-the-Hill, Chester, was to be embattled like the 'little closet' in Chester Castle; and the steeple of Helmingham church in Suffolk, construction of which was to be undertaken by Thomas Aldrych in 1487–8, was to be based on the steeples of Brandeston and Framsden. These clauses, which were no doubt inserted at the instigation of the patron, may suggest that copying was an accepted practice amongst medieval builders. It is unlikely, however, that it was ever intended that a building be reproduced exactly, and there can be considerable differences between a structure and its specified exemplar. This supports the view that in some cases models served only as a starting point in the process of design.

Masonic manuscripts

Foremost amongst the other masonic documents is the famous 'sketch-book' of Villard de Honnecourt. Villard was a native of Picardy who appears to have visited Chartres, Reims, Laon, Meaux, Switzerland and Hungary during the course of his career. Dating from the first half of the thirteenth century, this work comprises a series of drawings and notes illustrating the many aspects that a master mason might have been expected to take an interest in and which might have been of use to his craft. As well as architectural plans, elevations and details, it includes examples of practical geometry, masonry techniques, carpentry, mechanical devices (notably lifting machines) and sketches that could have been used as models for sculptures. Although the question of whether Villard was a practising mason has yet to be resolved, his sketch book is indicative of the breadth of understanding that a leading master mason had to encompass, and sits well with what we know of William of Sens's range of accomplishments.

For its time the sketchbook is unique, but it is supplemented by a collection of treatises by three late medieval German master masons. Mathes Roriczer's two works, *Buchlein von der Fialen Gerechtigkeit* ('Booklet on the correct design of pinnacles') and *Geometria Deutsch,* were published in Regensburg in 1486 and 1487 respectively. Hans Schmuttermayer of Nuremberg, a contemporary of Roriczer, was the author of a *Fialenbuchlein*, another booklet about the design of pinnacles, and in 1516 Lorenz Lechler compiled a book, known as his *Unterweisung* ('Instruction'), which was intended as a training manual for his son. These works also include examples of practical geometry and are useful for the information they give us about the medieval mason's design methods.

The appearance of these southern German texts towards the end of the Middle Ages denotes a desire to commit masonic techniques to writing. It may, therefore, be no coincidence that the Regensburg Statute dates from the same era. This is a list of rules that attempts to standardise the practice of masoncraft. In assessing its relevance for our period in general, it has to be said that it can only be held to be representative of late medieval convention in Germany and may not be applicable to an earlier time, when practice may have been more diverse. Even Villard's sketchbook dates from a period when most of the technical problems of the Gothic had been solved and innovation took the form of changes to decorative detail. It was only at this stage that masons felt able to catalogue the techniques of the craft.

3
Design

The role of the medieval master mason in design is often regarded as analogous to that of the modern architect. There is certainly a good deal to commend this view: the master mason was designer as well as builder. His knowledge of construction technology, allied with a grasp of geometry and a proficiency in drafting techniques, appears to place him on a similar level to that of his modern counterparts. As though to emphasise this role, contemporary illustrations often depict the master mason holding a pair of compasses and sometimes a square, the technical instruments that both symbolised and dignified his profession.

Geometry formed the basis of architectural design. It was used not only to construct details like arches, moulding profiles and tracery patterns but also for determining the forms and proportions of the buildings themselves. The sectional profiles of great churches were derived by constructing a geometrical figure, usually a square or an equilateral triangle, on a base whose length was equal to the width of the proposed building; the height of the nave was taken from that of the figure. The system based on the equilateral triangle was known as *ad triangulum*; it produced a building that was comparatively low in relation to its width (figure 3) and was much used by the Italian masters. An alternative system called *ad quadratum*, which was based on the square,

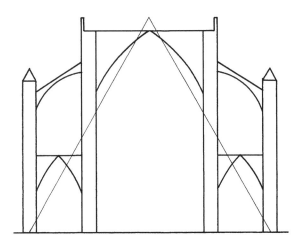

3. Section of a church designed *ad triangulum*.

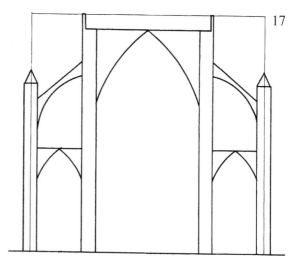

and which gave a greater height in relation to width (figure 4), was favoured by the more northerly builders of Gothic churches. This is the technical reason for many northern European cathedrals having greater verticality than their Italian counterparts.

In his sketchbook Villard de Honnecourt demonstrates a technique whereby a larger square could be created around a smaller one (figure 5), and Mathes Roriczer, in his *Buchlein von der Fialen Gerechtigkeit*, shows a method of creating a smaller square within a larger one (figure 5). In both cases this involves constructing the second square on a diagonal plane to the first and then rotating it so that the two squares are parallel. The sides of the larger square are equal to the diagonal of the smaller square, and the side of the smaller square is equal to half the diagonal of the larger. Villard's suggested application is to calculate the relative proportions of a cloister garth and its surrounding alleys. To Roriczer it was an invaluable tool in designing a pinnacle. A related technique was no doubt employed in the design of octagonal plans like those of King John's early-thirteenth-century great tower at Odiham Castle in Hampshire (figure 5), and of the late-thirteenth-century chapter-house of York Minster. The ground plans of these buildings were probably constructed by superimposing a second square at an angle of 45 degrees to the first.

In other cases the circle was the underlying figure. The quatrefoil plan of Clifford's Tower in York Castle, for instance, is a construction of four circles. Hexagonal buildings, like the late-fourteenth-century Old Wardour Castle in Wiltshire, are also derived from a circle through the division of the circumference into radius-length sections. Dividing it into half-radius lengths will give a twelve-sided figure like Caesar's

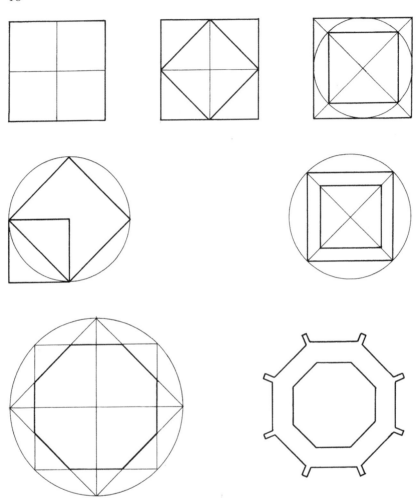

5. The manipulation of a square in medieval planning: (top) creating a smaller square from a larger; (centre) creating a larger square from a smaller; (bottom) creating an octagonal plan: Odiham Castle, Hampshire.

Tower at Warwick Castle. Some other circle-derived plans, like that of Orford Castle donjon in Suffolk, are more complex. T. A. Heslop has shown that the positions and widths of the three projecting turrets were determined by the manipulation of an equilateral triangle constructed within a circle, apparently using a technique that was later to be enshrined in Roriczer's *Geometria Deutsch*. This may seem complicated, but it

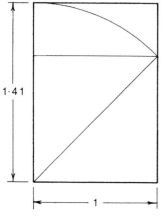

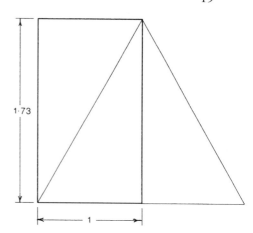

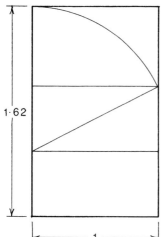

6. Some proportional systems used in the Middle Ages: (top left) one to the square root of two; (top right) one to the square root of three; (left) the golden section.

must be understood that the practical geometry of the medieval master mason required no understanding of mathematical principles, and was based on the prescribed manipulation of geometrical forms through the use of compass and square. It was technical rather than academic knowledge and was gained through a mastery of masonic tradition as opposed to formal schooling.

Also derived from geometry are the proportional systems of measurement that were widely used in medieval building design, like one to the square root of two, one to the square root of three, and the so called 'golden section' (figure 6). When expressed in such esoteric terms these systems appear to endow the 'mistery' of masoncraft with greater intellectual standing than it deserves. Here again it is necessary to stress that, to the medieval mason, they represented practical rather than theoretical training, a series of carefully stipulated steps rather than the application of mathematics. All were based on simple geometrical constructions: the square root three system was derived from the equilateral triangle and the golden section and the square root two systems from the square.

The most commonly used proportion, nowadays expressed as one to the square root of two, would have been understood by the master mason in terms of the relationship between the side of a square and its diagonal. Its use can be discerned in the ground plan of Lumley Castle, near Chester-le-Street, Durham, a symmetrical courtyard building raised by Sir Ralph Lumley between 1389 and 1400 (figure 7). The proportion is exemplified by the dimensions of the eastern corner towers, whose ground plans are based on a 35 foot (10.67 metre) square. The 35 foot (10.67 metre) width of the towers represents the side of the square, and the 49 foot 6 inch (15.08 metre) length its diagonal. The western towers are also 35 feet (10.67 metres) wide but are 64 feet (19.50 metres) long, dimensions that are products of the same proportional system, because 64 feet (19.50 metres) is equal to the 49 feet 6 inches (15.08 metres) of the eastern towers plus the difference between their width and length (14 feet 6 inches or 4.42 metres).

The size of the main block is related to the length of the eastern towers, since it appears to have been based on a grid of nine 49 foot 6 inch squares (148 feet 6 inches or 45.26 metres) (figure 7). The 105 foot (32 metre) distance between the east face of the east range and the east face of the west range is equal to half the diagonal of a 148 foot 6 inch (45.26 metre) square, and half the diagonal of a 105 foot (32 metre) square is 74 feet (22.55 metres), which is equal both to the width of the courtyard and to the internal lengths of the north and south ranges. Finally, a turret measuring 17 feet (5.18 metres) by 25 feet (7.62 metres) projected from the centre of the west range; these dimensions are also in the proportion of one to the square root of two, and this, too, is the relationship that 25 feet (7.62 metres) bears to 35 feet (10.67 metres).

Another part of the design process was the preparation of architectural drawings. A number of important survivals from the continent testify that the medieval architect was often a skilled draughtsman. Apart from Villard de Honnecourt's diagrams, thirteenth-century examples include elevations of the west front of Strasbourg Cathedral and of an unidentified church re-used as the pages of a book (the Reims palimpsest). Elevations of the cathedrals of Orvieto, Siena and Cologne date from the fourteenth century, and a design for the west tower of Ulm Minster is one of many

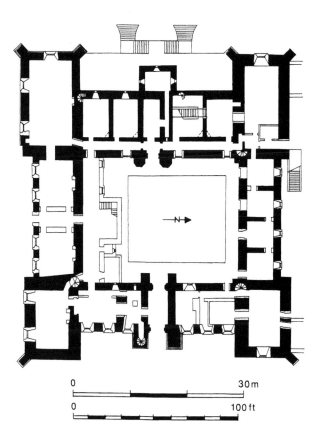

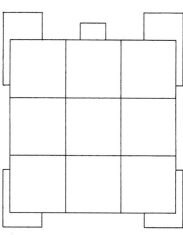

7. Lumley Castle, Durham: (above) ground plan; (right) the underlying proportions of the plan.

fifteenth-century subjects to be preserved on parchment. In contrast, comparable muniments from England are elusive: one fragment is a fourteenth-century drawing of a window, reused as a page in a late medieval sketchbook; another is of a tower, supposedly intended for King's College, Cambridge; but there is very little else. Although the extent of these vestiges may be disappointing, they are supplemented by numerous documentary references to the use of architectural drawings in England. One of the earliest of these dates from 1373, when the master mason Stephen Lomherst was to ensure that the tracery and moulded work of the new cloister at Boxley Abbey, Kent, complied with the forms and measurements of the 'moulds and drawings'. Later instances suggest that both plans and elevations were used. An unusual example of a mason's architectural sketch, dating from *c*.1280, was recovered from St John's College, Cambridge. It survived because it was inscribed on clunch and, after it had served its original purpose, was incorporated in the building. It shows a design for a window, apparently that of the east window of the chapel (figure 8).

These items appear to support the analogy between medieval and modern architects. It would, however, be a mistake to think of medieval

8. Sketch of a window design incised on stone with a pair of compasses *c*.1280, from St John's College, Cambridge. (University of Cambridge Museum of Archaeology and Anthropology)

9. Wenlock Priory, Much Wenlock, Shropshire. The squashed appearance of the southernmost bay of the south transept (left) represents a miscalculation on the part of the master mason.

masons' drawings in the same terms as modern architectural plans and elevations, from which the builder is able to reproduce the architect's design. Their primary purpose in the Middle Ages appears to have been to convey an impression of the mason's vision to the patron rather than to act as models for accurate reproduction. When the church of Wenlock Priory in Shropshire was rebuilt in the thirteenth century, the decision was made to incorporate the twelfth-century chapter-house in the new complex. The thirteenth-century south transept butts directly against this building and, although the transept's eastern arcade fits into the space available without any difficulty, in the south bay the twin arches of the triforium are squeezed up close together and are narrower than those of the other two bays (figure 9). The architect, in relying on ground-level measurements, possessed insufficient foresight to allow enough clearance for the upper storey. The result is a flawed design that could have been prevented had it been the practice to work from accurate and comprehensive drawings.

Indeed, the medieval architect's approach differed in one important essential from that of his modern counterpart: there is ample structural and documentary evidence to support the view that the design of a

10. Sheriff Hutton Castle, North Yorkshire, from the east. The building joints suggest that a change of plan occurred during the construction of the gatehouse and adjoining tower.

building was not finalised before building work began. Instead, it seems to have evolved as construction advanced. During the erection of the great tower of Knaresborough Castle, North Yorkshire, in the early fourteenth century, the master mason, Hugh de Tichemers, left the site on several occasions to consult the King, 'in order to find out his express wishes concerning the works', a clear sign that no detailed specification existed. Medieval buildings provide countless examples of evolving plans. A case in point is Sir Richard Scrope's late-fourteenth-century fortified mansion, whose remains can still be seen at Castle Bolton in Wensleydale, North Yorkshire. Two main structural phases can be discerned; the specifications for the earlier of these are enshrined in a contract of 1378, but an examination of the building itself shows that, whilst some of the dimensions correspond to those of the contract, there had been various changes of plan between the contract being drawn up and the beginning of building work.

At Sheriff Hutton Castle, near York (figure 10), the main entrance provides evidence for modifications to the original design. It is situated immediately north of, and flush with, the east face of the south-east corner tower. The masonry details, however, suggest that this was not the original intention and that a change of plan occurred while work was in progress. The building sequence can be stated thus: the ground storey of the south-east tower was built first, and it appears that the gateway was intended to be recessed, for the lower part of the tower's east face, immediately south of the entrance, was provided with quoins, indicating that at this point it returned to the west. Then there was a change of plan and the gateway was begun, or modified, being built up against the quoins of the tower. When the gateway had reached a height equal to that of the partly built tower, the gateway and tower were carried up together in continuous courses so that the final external appearance would have been that of a gatehouse tower pierced by an entrance at its north end.

In conclusion, while it is certainly justified that the architectural role of the medieval master mason should be given due prominence, we are also bound to recognise that there was a fundamental difference between the ways in which he and his modern counterpart approached design. In the Middle Ages, design was not the detached occupation that it is today. Owing, perhaps, to the practical nature of masonic training, it progressed in stages, was in some measure empirical, and marched hand in hand with the process of construction.

4
Preparation

Quarrying

In the early stages of preparation for construction it was necessary to obtain a supply of stone. Owing to the difficulties and expense of transporting building materials it was desirable to establish a quarry as close as possible to the site. Many building sites could provide a source of lower-quality material for the walls but most did not possess suitable stone for ashlar blocks and dressings. Sometimes the patron would provide a quarry for the mason to work, but in other cases stone might have to be procured from stone merchants or from independent quarry masters who acted as suppliers to numerous building works.

One good-quality stone used extensively in the East Midlands and East Anglia during the Middle Ages came from Barnack in Cambridgeshire, where an industrial landscape known as the 'Hills and Holes' has been created by the activities of the medieval quarriers (figure 11). It comprises a series of shallow pits and spoil heaps and serves as a reminder that the usual method of quarrying in the Middle

11. The 'Hills and Holes', Barnack, Cambridgeshire; a medieval industrial landscape created by quarrying. (© Crown Copyright/MOD. Reproduced with permission of the Controller of Her Majesty's Stationery Office.)

12. Beeston Castle, Cheshire; tooling marks made by the quarriers of the inner ditch: (top) abandoned vertical wedge holes (viewed from above); (above) abandoned horizontal wedge holes; (left) wedge marks at the edge of the ditch.

Ages was to clear the overlying earth from a strip of ground and to excavate the bedrock to a limited depth within a confined area.

The technique is illustrated by a number of excavated examples. A roofing-slate quarry, uncovered within the deserted medieval settlement of Hillam Burchard in Lincolnshire, was roughly rectangular and measured 9 metres by 5 metres and was between 0.2 metres and 0.5 metres deep. There were indications that the stone had been cut out in 1.5 metre square blocks and lifted with the aid of a crane situated on the edge of the excavation. At Burystead, near Raunds in Northamptonshire, a group of seven quarries has been investigated. The largest were similar in length and width to the Hillam Burchard working but all were deeper, ranging from 2 metres to 2.1 metres, and were provided with access steps or ramps.

Other types of quarrying were practised in the Raunds area during the Middle Ages, including much shallower and less well defined excavations for the extraction of limestone rubble and the exploitation of hillside outcrops. Occasionally, man-made features associated with the buildings themselves served as quarries: the rock-cut ditch that isolates the inner ward of Beeston Castle in Cheshire, for instance, was evidently the source for much of the walling material used in this part of the castle. A close examination of the Beeston ditch reveals a number of tooling marks, which provide evidence for the method of extraction (figure 12). The rock was split, both vertically and horizontally, by

13. St Albans Abbey, Hertfordshire: reused Roman columns from *Verulamium*.

hammering lines of wedges into it.

Ancient buildings provided another source of stone, particularly in the early Middle Ages. The late-eleventh-century St Albans Abbey is largely built of material from the adjacent Roman town of *Verulamium*, and the builders of the Anglo-Norman cathedral of York used both Roman masonry, from the surrounding legionary fortress, and Anglo-Saxon material from the site of an earlier church. Such reuse is more usually recognisable in the foundations but, although distinguishable features were normally obliterated above ground level, good-quality masonry sometimes retained its original form. At St Albans the triforium of the south transept incorporates recognisable Roman columns (figure 13), whereas some of the stones in the Anglo-Saxon church of St Eata at Atcham in Shropshire retain marks that identify the masonry as second-hand material, made for a different purpose (figure 14), which probably came from the nearby Roman town of *Viroconium* at Wroxeter. In addition, there is some evidence to suggest that occasionally Roman features were employed in the capacity for which they were designed. A small number of Anglo-Saxon churches, including St Peter at Barton-on-Humber, North Lincolnshire, appear to contain entire Roman arches, removed from their original locations and reset.

The recycling of building stone also appears to have been common practice later in the Middle Ages. A considerable number of sculptural fragments made in the twelfth century for York Minster were recovered during the excavations of the nearby College of the Vicars Choral, where they had been used as building rubble. It is evident, too, from several building contracts that where a new building was replacing an earlier one it was not unusual to reuse the earlier material. In 1383, when the master mason Henry Holme undertook to build a new gatehouse at Dunstanburgh Castle in Northumberland, it was agreed that he would reuse the voussoirs, jambs and barbicans of the old gatehouse, which was thereafter blocked and converted into a great tower. Henry Middleton, who contracted to demolish and rebuild the monks' dormitory at Durham Priory in 1398, was to have all the stone from the old work and was to rework the old windows.

Mortar

Preparation of lime mortar began by obtaining chalk or limestone and burning it in kilns specially prepared for the purpose. Occasionally the activities of the medieval lime-burners are brought to light by archaeology. One concern appears to have operated from Beadnell Point on the coast of Northumberland, where the archaeological excavation of a medieval lime-kiln demonstrated that it had been in service for a considerable period before going out of use in the late fifteenth or early

Medieval Masons

14. Church of St Eata, Atcham, Shropshire; reused Roman work: (left) part of a sculptured relief; (below) a possible lewis hole. (A lewis was a device for lifting stone.)

sixteenth century.

After burning the chalk or limestone to produce quicklime, and slaking it with water to produce lime putty, sand was added and mortar produced in a mechanical mixer. Mortar mixers have been reconstructed using evidence from archaeological excavation. Three examples, for instance, have been excavated at Northampton, next to the church of St Peter. They appear to have comprised a circular well set into the ground, with a central post that supported, and acted as a pivot for, a horizontal beam to which a number of paddles were attached. When the beam was turned the paddles agitated the mortar.

Transport of materials

Where local supplies were not available the transport of materials became one of the medieval builder's major concerns. Great attention is paid to the subject in the building contracts: responsibility for transport was always made explicit, sometimes to the point of pedantry. At Stafford Castle, Ralph Lord Stafford was to transport the stone, sand and lime to the foot of the motte, but the master mason, John of Burcestre, was responsible for carrying it to the top of the motte. Such apparent niceties, however, had an important bearing on the cost of a project, because transport was a major source of expenditure. At Caernarvon Castle the total amount spent on materials in 1285–6 was £151 5s 6$\frac{1}{2}$d but the cost of transportation was £535 8s 8$\frac{1}{2}$d.

There are numerous references in the building accounts to transport of stone in carts, but road travel was slow, cumbersome and expensive. Where the site was close to navigable waters, transport by boat was often a more feasible and cost-effective option. William of Sens's importation of Caen stone has already been mentioned, but the building accounts of the royal works are full of references to the transport of stone by water.

One of the main problems posed by the construction of Rievaulx Abbey in North Yorkshire was its situation in the 'wilderness' and the lack of an adequate transport system to bring in the materials. The solution of the Cistercians was inventive and influenced by the evident advantages of water transport. Canals were constructed along the valley for the express purpose of moving the materials to the building site. The stone, which was obtained from hillside quarries, was brought down to the valley floor on wooden sledges to specially constructed wharves and thence floated to the abbey.

Lifting machinery

The height of many medieval buildings and the weight of the individual stones from which they were constructed leads to speculation about the methods by which the masonry was raised and manoeuvred into position. Contemporary illustrations depict various mechanical devices for lifting stone and other materials, involving jibs and pulleys and based on the windlass principle, whereby the turning of a wheel allowed materials to be raised by means of a cable attached to its horizontal axle. These machines range from the treadmill, in which a great wheel was turned by one or more operators walking round inside it, to the hand winch, which was sufficient for smaller loads. Medieval windlasses survive at Tewkesbury Abbey and Salisbury Cathedral, and a particularly well-preserved machine, dating from the thirteenth century, exists in the north-west tower of Peterborough Cathedral (figure 15). The wheel has a diameter of over 3.66 metres and is fitted with a series of rungs. These project on either side of the rim and form handles or steps on which the operators could gain purchase in order to turn the machine.

Preparation of details

In between establishing a quarry and commencing building work, the stonecutters had to be supplied with patterns from which to work. The method whereby designs of architectural detailing, including mouldings and window tracery, were reproduced in stone was simple but effective. Using compasses and square, the master mason drew them out at full

15. A thirteenth-century windlass in the north-west tower of Peterborough Cathedral. (By permission of the Dean and Chapter)

16. Sculpture of
c.1330–40 depicting a
mason using a hammer
and chisel. (The
Yorkshire Museum,
York; photograph by
Dr Christopher
Wilson)

size on specially prepared plaster floor surfaces, a process that is vividly illustrated at York Minster, where one of the few surviving medieval 'tracing floors' is preserved. On the York tracing floor, where there are several generations of superimposed drawings, the design of *c*.1360 for the window tracery of the Lady Chapel aisles has been recognised and found to correspond exactly with its execution. Once he had set out the designs, the master mason used them as patterns from which to make a series of wooden templates or 'moulds', which he then delivered to the stonecutters. The stonecutter squared his block of stone to size, inscribed the profile of the template on each end of it and then cut it to shape. The process can be readily imagined from the examination of a moulding section (figure 17), but those pieces of carved work that are shaped in more than one plane appear more problematic. An interesting piece of evidence, however, is provided by a thirteenth-century double capital

17. A thirteenth-century moulded stone from Croxden Abbey, Staffordshire.

recovered during excavations at St Mary's Abbey, York (figure 19). It shows that a similar technique was used for this three-dimensional work. Not only would a template have been used to inscribe the horizontal profile of the uppermost section, but the upper surface of the capital also retains the inscribed moulding patterns of the capital's intermediate and lower sections.

Setting out the plan

The construction process began by clearing the site and marking out

18. A section of dog-tooth moulding from St Mary's Abbey, York.

19. Double capital from St Mary's Abbey, York, showing the mason's setting-out lines. (The Yorkshire Museum, York; photograph by Dr Christopher Wilson.)

the plan of the building on the ground with a series of wooden pegs. The first step would be to mark the position of one of the corners. Cords could then be run out at right angles from the corner peg to represent the walls. The right angle itself could be established using the principle of the 3:4:5 triangle, whereby the angle opposite the longest side is always a right angle. In practical terms this would mean using cord to set out a triangle on the ground with sides in the proportion of 3:4:5, the hypotenuse being opposite the corner peg. Further pegs would be established to mark other wall angles and junctions. Archaeological evidence for the technique comes from Germany: the excavators of Rickenbach Castle discovered the square-sectioned stake hole from a corner peg at the internal angle of one of the buildings. Geometrical shapes were constructed in a similar fashion, with a series of pegs and cord substituting for the compasses used in the design process. At York Minster in the 1930s excavations in the Anglo-Norman crypt revealed the setting-out peg that served as the centre from which the semi-circular curve of the apse was struck.

Foundations

Once the building plan had been laid out, the foundation trenches could be excavated and the foundation requirements assessed. Experience taught medieval builders to recognise the importance of good foundations, especially where the ground was inclined to be unstable. The failure in the late tenth century of Ramsey Abbey tower in the Cambridgeshire fens was attributed to 'too weak a foundation'. The tower was taken down and the foundations remade 'with a mass of stones more firmly compacted with pounding of rams and with tough mortar'. At the royal manor of Eltham, south-east London, a team of masons was engaged in 1315 to build a wall around the edge of the moat on potentially marshy land. The contract, drawn up on the advice of the consultant mason, Master Michael of Canterbury, stipulated that the foundation was to be of 'good hard stone' and that, if firm ground could not be found, the footings were to be built on wooden piles.

This is one of the many references to the use of piling and there is no doubt that it was common practice on sites of doubtful stability. Timber was also used in foundation work in other ways. At Winchester Cathedral a timber raft was constructed to support part of the eastern arm of the church, and at Richmond Castle, North Yorkshire, substantial timbers were incorporated into the eleventh-century stone wall in order to prevent slippage. The Richmond work is contemporary with the Anglo-Norman Minster of York, where timber reinforcements of a different kind were used in the foundations. Here the foundation trenches were excavated to a depth of 6 feet (1.82 metres), but deeper exploratory pits were also dug at intervals along them in an attempt to ascertain the underlying nature of the site. The results of these investigative excavations, which revealed that the ground was unreliable in parts, probably influenced the character of the foundations. Firstly, the trenches were partially filled with a layer of ready-mixed, mortared rubble, 2 feet 6 inches (0.76 metre) thick. On top of this layer the builders erected a two-tier timberwork grid, the longitudinal members of which were scarf-jointed together to form continuous lengths. Retaining walls were raised on either side of the trench to just below ground level and the area between them, including the spaces between the timbers, was filled with more mortared rubble. This formed the foundation on which the walls of the church were built. The purpose of this unusual timber grid may have been to prevent the uneven settlement of the footings over the lengthy period it took the mortar to set.

5
Construction

Character of masonry

Many medieval walls were composite structures in which the inner and outer faces were built up simultaneously, the gap between them being filled with mortared rubble. The technique is illustrated in buildings in which the facing stone has been stripped from the walls to reveal the rubble core (figure 20). The facings fall into two principal categories, rubble and ashlar. Rubble appears in the documents as 'rough walling' and was a cheaper type of construction, comprising stones of irregular shape and size. It required a less skilled workforce than did ashlar walling, which consisted of good-quality dressed stone blocks of regular shape and size, often finely jointed. At the late-twelfth-century castle of Conisbrough in South Yorkshire the two contrasting types of masonry can be seen in juxtaposition (figure 21). Good-quality ashlar was used for the donjon, whereas the curtain wall was built of rubble. Sometimes both types of masonry were used in the same building, ashlar for the exterior, in order to enhance the outward prestige of the building, and rubble for the interior, to reduce cost. Most surviving Anglo-Saxon

20. Lilleshall Abbey, Shropshire. The robbing of the facing stones from the walls has revealed the rubble core.

21. Conisbrough Castle, South Yorkshire: the ashlar keep and rubble curtain wall.

buildings are built of rubble walling, though ashlar work does occur at the Anglo-Saxon church of St Lawrence at Bradford-on-Avon in Wiltshire, and the technique may have been more common before the Norman Conquest than is now apparent.

Other recognisable types exist that share some, though not all, of the characteristics of one or both of these main categories. In the keep of *c*.1068 at Chepstow Castle, Monmouth-shire, the masonry consisted of small, square, regularly coursed blocks, a technique that was used in northern France in the tenth and eleventh centuries (figure 22) and seems to have been derived ultimately from Roman building methods. One particularly distinctive kind of stonework, usually associated with the eleventh century, is known as herringbone masonry. In this technique the stones are set obliquely, so that the direction of pitch alternates from course to course in order to provide a system of counterbalance. The resultant 'herringbone' patterns were interspersed with horizontal levelling courses of thin flat stones. Herringbone masonry is found in a number of Anglo-Saxon churches but was also used in early Norman work and is not necessarily confined to the eleventh century. The late Professor Hamilton Thompson's view that it was a method to be used when speed was required is recommended by its repeated occurrence in early castles such as Exeter (Devon) and Peak (Derbyshire), both thrown up hastily in the midst of a hostile populace. The quality of work varies enormously, but the inner bailey wall of Tamworth Castle, Staffordshire, is a particularly accomplished example (figure 23).

22. Château de Langeais, Indre et Loire, France: eleventh-century masonry.

23. The inner bailey wall of Tamworth Castle, Staffordshire: an example of herringbone masonry.

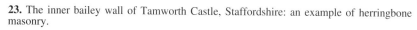

24. Carreg Cennan, Carmarthenshire: horizontal building breaks denoting successive building seasons. Note that darker stonework was used for the first season's work than for the second and that the masonry of the second and third seasons is divided by a narrow levelling course. The leaching that disfigures the lower part of the wall starts at this level.

Building joints

Building was essentially a seasonal occupation lasting for about six months of the year. As we have seen, at the end of the season the unfinished walls were covered over in order to protect them from the destructive effects of water and frost. In the case of rubble walling this annual hiatus gave rise to a series of clearly discernible horizontal breaks (figure 24). These may occasionally be identified by a double thickness of mortar, a feature that represents a protective capping given to the wall at the end of one year's season and the first application at the beginning of the next. Such seasonal breaks may also be accentuated by differences in the character of the masonry resulting from changes in technique, sources of stone, or style.

On the basis of detailed analyses of building fabrics, Dr Warwick Rodwell has proposed that rubble walls rose at a daily rate of 0.2–0.5 metre. Contrasting with this is the documentary evidence suggesting that medieval buildings rose by an average height of between 10 feet (3.04 metres) and 12 feet (3.66 metres) a year. Obviously the rate of

25. Caernarvon Castle, Gwynedd. Lines of projecting stones or tusks in the rear wall of the King's Gate (either side of the archway and to the extreme right of the building) mark the positions of walls that were part of the original plan but which were never built.

progress had much to do with the size of the building and the strength of the workforce. The use of lime mortar may, however, have been a contributory factor: its notoriously slow setting time may have made it dangerous to proceed beyond a certain height. It is certainly true that the stability of newly built or partially completed walls was questionable. We have seen, for instance, that the partially built west front of St Albans Abbey church collapsed because the walls were left uncovered during the 'rainy season'.

In addition to giving us clues to the rate of upward progress, building joints can also indicate the lateral sequence of construction. The building contract of 1412 for the Church of St Anne at Catterick, North Yorkshire, explicitly excludes the vestry and the tower but nevertheless provides for their subsequent erection. It stipulates that the master mason is to prepare the appropriate areas of the new church walls to receive these elements at a later date by leaving stone toothing projecting from the completed walls, the objective being to facilitate bonding when the vestry and tower were finally erected. The technique can be seen at Caernarvon Castle, Gwynedd, where provision was made for a structural division between the east and west wards immediately south of the King's Gate (figure 25). This was never completed, but the intention of the builders is clear from an examination of the fabric.

In addition to the joints between the articulated components of a structure, vertical breaks sometimes occur within an apparently integrated

42

26. Bolton Castle, Wensleydale, North Yorkshire. The vertical joint between the two phases of the south range is immediately to the left of the left-hand transomed window.

building. It is not always easy to determine the chronological relationship between two such phases. Bolton Castle, North Yorkshire, has already been mentioned in this context (figure 26). Here one of the indications that the western part of the south range was built after the eastern part is to be found inside the range. The wall between the two phases is of double thickness, the second thickness having been built in order to provide an abutment for the tunnel vaulting of the later phase. Such vertical breaks are evidence for carefully planned phased construction, possibly resulting from limits on annual expenditure. According to the sixteenth-century antiquary John Leland, the expenditure on Bolton Castle amounted to 1000 marks per annum, a circumstance that is suggestive of the work

27. Lilleshall Abbey, Shropshire: the vertical joint between the two phases of the nave.

having been carefully budgeted. In less systematically planned operations, or where the family affairs and finances were erratic, work may have been completed as and when economic or other circumstances permitted.

The nave of a great church was often of two different structural phases, and this is emphasised where there was a long hiatus between periods of building activity. Henry III's reconstruction of Westminster Abbey, for example, carried out between 1245 and 1272, included the eastern arm, crossing, transepts and the first few bays of the nave, but work on the nave was not resumed until the reign of Richard II (1377–99). At Lilleshall Abbey, Shropshire, the two phases are marked by a vertical joint between the first and second bays of the nave and are highlighted by a distinct change in the character of the masonry (figure 27). That of the eastern bay, which contains a highly decorated processional doorway of *c*.1160–70, consists of squared and coursed blocks. That in the next phase is less regular, for, although it contains stones of similar size to the earlier masonry, these are more roughly worked and are interspersed with small levelling stones. The nave can be dated to *c*.1190–1200 from its Transitional capitals.

The construction of a great church usually began at the east end so that it might be brought into religious use as soon as possible. The

28. Worcester Cathedral. The nave wall incorporates flying buttresses that cut across the openings of the clerestory and triforium. They provide extra support for the crossing.

important elements were the presbytery and the choir. The choir might be situated in the eastern arm or might extend into the crossing or even into the structural nave, so its position might have influenced the extent of the first phase. Regardless of the position of the choir, however, wherever the crossing did form part of the construction phase the transepts and at least the first bay of the nave were usually included as well in order to serve as buttresses to the crossing. This buttressing function of the nave occurs at the cathedrals of Chester and Durham and is shown particularly clearly at Worcester, where the eastern bay of the nave incorporates flying buttresses (figure 28). Similar features are to be found in the transept of Gloucester Cathedral.

Not all irregularities in the jointing of ashlar work relate to the sequential development of the building. The masons faced special problems where features like windows, doorways and fireplaces were to be incorporated into the fabric. Window surrounds, for example, were cut from stones of different length and width in order to facilitate bonding with the adjacent masonry; where they are arched it may have been necessary to accommodate voussoirs. The result can be untidy, contrasting strongly with the regularity of the surrounding walls and giving the erroneous impression that the features have been inserted into an existing building. These instances indicate that some cutting work was carried out on site, as the layers were at work (figure 29).

29. Wressle Castle, East Yorkshire. Steps have been cut into the window jambs in order to accommodate the surrounding stonework.

30. Wingfield Manor House, Derbyshire: a narrow 'closer' used to infill between two larger stones.

Apart from the irregularities that occur around openings, ashlar walls sometimes contain stones that are noticeably narrower than the other component blocks. These 'closers' (figure 30) may indicate that more than one mason layer worked on the same length of wall at the same time. They represent stones cut specially to size in order to fill the gaps where two sections of work meet.

Scaffolding techniques

Scaffolding is depicted in a number of medieval illustrations. The platforms on which the masons stood were hurdles, rectangular frames of interwoven withies, which had the advantages of being both light and strong. They were supported on a series of horizontal scaffolding poles or putlogs. These were either cantilevered out from the walls on raking supports or tied to vertical posts, so that the whole arrangement resembled conventional modern scaffolding. Putlog holes are amongst the most common surviving indications of construction methods. These square apertures (figure 31), which indicate the positions of the putlogs, often form regular linear networks. The horizontal rows are commonly 1.5 metres apart, a distance that represents the height of walling that a mason could comfortably complete from a standing position. The pattern varies on cylindrical towers where they are sometimes found in helical patterns (figure 31). Remains of putlogs have occasionally been discovered in putlog holes, evidence that they were cut off flush with the wall when they could not be easily removed. Dr Rodwell has drawn attention to examples found in the Saxon churches of Deerhurst (Gloucestershire) and Brixworth (Northamptonshire).

31. Harlech Castle, Gwynedd: (above) a putlog hole; (below) putlog holes in a helical pattern.

Lintel, arch and vault construction

Walling is straightforward to build; spanning open spaces is more problematic. The simplest method is to use a lintel. Lintels were used in the construction of windows, doorways and fireplaces. Their disadvantage is that they have to take the full strain of the wall above them, and relieving arches were often built over them to disperse the load. Support was sometimes provided by corbels; the most distinctive

32. (Above left) Caernarvon Castle, Gwynedd: a Caernarvon arch. Note that the left-hand corbel has failed immediately below the edge of the lintel.

33. (Above right) Conisbrough Castle, South Yorkshire: joggled lintel over the entrance to the keep.

type of corbel and lintel construction is the Caernarvon arch (figure 32), which incorporates corbels with concave profiles. It came into popularity in the 1240s, was widely used at Caernarvon Castle in the late thirteenth century, whence it takes its name, and continued in use down to about 1400. The same structural principle is used to support the stone slab ceilings that are sometimes found in passageways as an alternative to vaulting. The most accomplished and beautiful examples of lintels, however, are those which are composed of several pieces of masonry held together with joggled joints (figure 33). The technique came into use around the middle of the twelfth century and was used throughout the Middle Ages, most often in the construction of fireplaces.

The most easily assembled arches were those in which each half was formed by a single stone (figure 34). The technique is more often, though not exclusively, associated with narrow openings, where there is minimal overhang. Normally, however, arches were made up of a series of voussoirs, with or without keystones (figure 35), and it was

34. (Above left) Bolton Castle, North Yorkshire: an arch formed of two stones.

35. (Above right) Carlisle Castle, Cumbria: an arch in the outer gatehouse formed of voussoirs, including a keystone at the apex.

necessary to build them on wooden centring. These supportive frameworks held the masonry in position until the arches became self-supporting. Occasionally a contemporary drawing depicts the use of centring for constructing a door or window arch but archaeological evidence tends to be lacking. Both types of arch are found in the donjon of Warkworth Castle, Northumberland. In one example, in which the two voussoirs at the apex of the arch did not quite meet at the centre, the masons used oyster shells at the point of juncture to fill the gap between them (figure 36).

The simplest type of vault is the tunnel vault, in which a space is roofed by a simple arched structure springing from the side walls. While it was being built, the vault had to be supported by a substantial wooden infrastructure. At Belsay Castle in Northumberland, transverse masonry joints indicate that the tunnel vaulting of the tower-house basement was made in a series of short lengths rather than all at once. This technique, which has also been recognised in Scotland, may have facilitated the

36. Warkworth Castle donjon, Northumberland: oyster shells used for levelling voussoirs.

removal of the centring after construction, thereby allowing it to be reused.

One technique of tunnel-vault construction that can be recreated from archaeological evidence is that in which the centring carried a series of planks on which a layer of mortar and rubble was built up. When the mortar had set the centring was removed, leaving the impressions of the planks on the roof of the vault. At Lincoln Cathedral, in the staircase chamber of the north-east transept, when the centring was removed some of the planks adhered to the mortar and were retained *in situ*.

Tunnel vaulting presents few problems about the working methods of the medieval master mason. In high rib vaulting, however, where the skeleton of ribs that formed the basis of the structure was infilled with panels of stone webbing on several curving planes, the techniques of construction have still to be worked out in detail. Not only must the masons have faced great technical challenges, they have left very little evidence about their methods. Massive works of centring and formwork must have been supported on a scaffolding arrangement at the level from which the vaulting ribs sprang. It was from this level, when engaged in 'preparing with machines for the turning of the great vault', that the master mason William of Sens suffered a crippling fall after the scaffolding on which he was standing collapsed. This is the closest we come to a contemporary description of vault construction.

6
Identifying the work of individual masons

Masons' marks

A topic that has engendered considerable interest over the years is the extent to which architecture can be identified as the work of individual master masons. Masons' marks (figure 37), which are sometimes used as a source for interpreting the construction history of a building, are one way of identifying the individuals who worked on the project. In most cases these personal identification marks were placed on finely worked stones, by the masons who shaped them, for purposes of quality control and calculation of payments; occasionally marks were inscribed by those who dressed the masonry so that it fitted firmly into its allocated position.

Masons' marks can be related to individuals. Many, however, are simple and widely used: triangles and crosses, including swastikas, were favourites. In some buildings there are only slight variations between some of the marks, and it has been suggested that these related marks belonged to the members of a team of masons assembled for the duration of a project. In such circumstances a mason might be only temporarily identified with a specific mark.

Occasionally, however, one comes across an unusually well formed or original mark that leads one to speculate that the perpetrator was a man of greater than average account. Some of these were clearly related to the mason's name. Thomas Crump, for example, used the letter 'T' as his mark. It appears on his seal attached to the contract of 1381 for the gatehouse at Cooling Castle, Kent (figure 2).

Corroborative evidence that masons' marks can sometimes represent extraordinary individuals is provided by marks in the north aisle of Beverley Minster, East Yorkshire, that are accompanied by graffiti in the form of personal names. One graffito, 'Maltun', has been taken as evidence that William Malton, who became master mason of Beverley Minster in 1335, had previously worked as a stonecutter there. This, however, is probably the only case so far in which a mason's mark has been related to a known individual.

Stylistic analysis

Perhaps the greatest single contribution to the subject of attribution to individual architects has been made by John Harvey, who in his pioneering work *English Mediaeval Architects,* first published in 1952, created a biographical dictionary of master masons and carpenters. However, whilst numerous documentary references link individual master masons to specific buildings, seldom are they sufficient to recreate more than a portion of a mason's career. Comparative stylistic analysis is required between the documented works and contemporaneous structures in order to fill some of the gaps.

The method for identifying the works of an individual is based on the premise that buildings by the same architect are likely to contain similar elements or combinations of elements. The investigator notes the characteristic features of a known work or works and then tries to find parallels within unattributed contemporary buildings. Proof that the system is viable is provided by the case of Master Thomas of Witney, who is known from documentary evidence to have worked at the cathedrals of Winchester, Wells and Exeter during the early fourteenth century. In this instance, Dr Richard Morris has described a distinctive style from which he has been able to argue that, even had there been no historical record of Master Thomas's connection with Exeter, it would

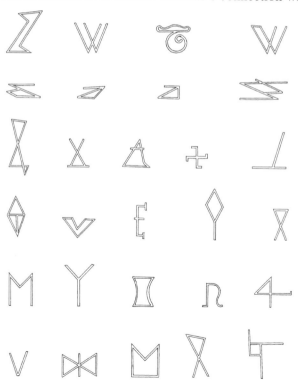

37. Some fourteenth-century masons' marks.

Medieval Masons

still have been possible to trace his involvement through a study of the architecture.

The process is not without its difficulties. We know, for instance, that copying was widespread in the Middle Ages. The fact that several building contracts stipulate that some of the work was to be based on existing models suggests that this was often at the behest of the patron. Some areas of design were more susceptible to external influence than others. Window tracery was one aspect of a building on which the patron sometimes insisted on having his say. When the contract for rebuilding the monks' dormitory at Durham Priory was drawn up in 1398 the master mason, Henry Middleton, was referred to a number of exemplars for the designs of the side windows, mostly from within the priory itself, whereas the great south window was to be made 'according to the will and dictate' of the prior. The tracery pattern used for the upper windows is also found at Lumley Castle near Durham (1389–1400), but its ultimate source appears to be a late-fourteenth-century design made by the master mason William Wynford for Winchester College (1387) and Wells Cathedral. Wynford's design may have been transferred to Durham by Walter Skirlaw, Bishop of Bath and Wells (1386–8) and then of Durham (1388–1407).

If window tracery might sometimes be suspect in identifying a specific mason's work, moulding profiles are thought to be more certain to reflect the choice of the master mason. One must, however, consider the possibility that mouldings were purchased from the quarries already formed and that their design owed nothing to the master mason on site.

Where there is a complete dearth of historical data, stylistic analysis can be used to establish the existence of anonymous individuals or of 'schools' based on regional traditions. In recent years a number of regional studies have been carried out which illuminate the process and the degree of probability evinced by the results.

Some interesting evidence comes from Dr Richard Fawcett's work in Norfolk. Particularly striking parallels have been drawn between both the mouldings and the window tracery of a group of mid-fourteenth-century churches, including that of Great Walsingham (figure 38). The analogies are sufficiently close to suggest the reuse of moulding templates in different buildings. The corollary of this discovery is that we are dealing with an individual architect and his personal set of templates rather than a school based on regional practices.

Dr Fawcett has drawn similar conclusions from the affinities between a collection of mid-fifteenth-century churches, which includes the church of St Mary at Wiveton. An interesting sidelight to the research, however, is that the diverse character of the details in some of these churches suggests that more than one mason had responsibility for design. The

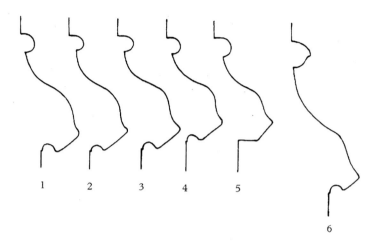

38. Mouldings by the architect of Great Walsingham church, Norfolk. (Above) Plinth courses: 1 Beetley; 2 Little Fransham; 3 Beeston; 4 Great Walsingham; 5 Houghton; 6 Tunstead. (Below) Piers and responds: 1 Little Fransham; 2 Tunstead; 3 Walsingham; 4 Beeston; 5 Narborough; 6 Beetley. (Dr Richard Fawcett and the Norwich and Norfolk Archaeological Society)

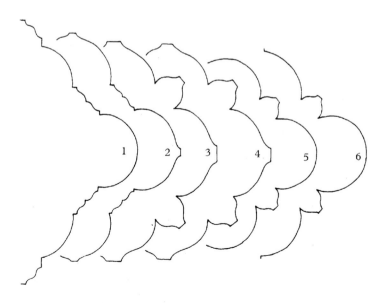

phenomenon has been recognised elsewhere: the sixteenth-century tower house of Hillslap, near Galashiels in the Scottish Borders, for example, displays two distinct types of architectural detail, suggesting that both Scottish and English masons worked on the building. In Norfolk the contrast of styles is interpreted as a succession of masons and an interrupted building sequence, but at Hillslap there is clear structural evidence that the builders responsible for both types of detail were employed simultaneously. Chippings from the freestone were incorporated in the rubble walls of the building, an indication that the dressed stone was cut on site.

This leads us to the question of delegation. The evidence from Hillslap suggests that the freemasons sometimes had a degree of independence in the sphere of design. Even where documentary evidence exists it will seldom be sufficiently unambiguous to elucidate such niceties. It is not entirely clear, for instance, whether Master Thomas of Witney was the designer of the characteristic detailing with which he is linked or whether he may have had an associate to whom he delegated such aspects.

Paradoxically, where the reconstruction of a mason's career is based very much upon written evidence, a stylistic comparison can seem less than convincing. Numerous documentary references, for example, underpin the attribution of a large corpus of building works to the later fourteenth-century mason Henry Yevele (figure 39). These have been augmented by circumstantial evidence and an element of comparative

39. A vaulting boss in the cloisters of Canterbury Cathedral believed to be a portrait of the fourteenth-century master mason Henry Yevele.

analysis to suggest that Yevele was the dominant figure in the south-east of England over a period of some thirty years.

Yevele is one of a number of master masons with large practices who had concurrent responsibility for several building projects. The works associated with him, however, do not form a coherent stylistic group, and it is arguable as to whether they would have been bracketed together had the documentary references not existed. Yevele's name is associated with those of other craftsmen in many of these projects, a circumstance that has led to the suggestion that his role was primarily that of co-ordinator rather than architect.

An alternative explanation for the disparate nature of his attributed works, however, might lie in the size of his practice. In a large practice, there would have been greater need for delegation than in circumstances in which the mason could devote his whole attention to one project. The degree of autonomy given to a deputy or subcontractor might have affected the interpretation of the design. In such cases moulding analysis might have little relevance to the identification of an individual or school.

This is certainly true in the case of Master James of St Georges, the architectural mastermind behind the series of late-thirteenth-century castles erected by Edward I in North Wales. Notwithstanding that each building had its own individuality, and many their own resident master mason, certain features point to the overall control of a single architect. The segment-headed windows and polychrome masonry that have been highlighted as some of the distinguishing features of Master James's work are aspects of the design that might well have been dictated by the patron. In this case, however, it is known that Master James had used them previously, when he was in the service of the Duke of Savoy. Most telling of all, perhaps, is the positioning of the garderobe turrets adjacent to the corner towers at Harlech (figure 40) and Rhuddlan (figure 41). This feature, which is also found in Savoy at castles associated with Master James, is an aspect of general planning that is likely to have emanated only from the mind of the master mason.

Further support for the view that some master masons delegated responsibility for design has been afforded by a study of a late-fourteenth-century Durham master mason, John Lewyn. Lewyn's documented works are widely distributed over an area that includes the ancient counties of York, Durham, Cumberland, Northumberland and Roxburgh. Within this region there are several regional schools of masoncraft, each with its own distinct characteristics, contributing to considerable differences in decorative detailing. One of the main arguments in linking many buildings to Lewyn, however, was based on affinities in planning that transcend these regional schools. In these circumstances the study

40. Harlech Castle, Gwynedd: tower and garderobe turret.

of mouldings or window tracery will be of limited usefulness. There is, for example, a marked relationship between the internal plans of Lewyn's main surviving work, Bolton Castle, North Yorkshire, and a number of slightly later castles. Of particular interest is the way in which comparable accommodation at Bolton and the donjon of Warkworth Castle, Northumberland, has been laid out within buildings of quite different ground plan. There is no doubt that the architect of Warkworth must have had an intimate knowledge and understanding of Bolton's labyrinthine internal plan. The most probable explanation is that the same man was involved in creation of both buildings.

Apart from internal planning, there are various other distinguishing features that contribute to the argument. One is a series of unusual flues built into the heads of some of the windows at the castles of Warkworth,

41. Rhuddlan Castle, Denbighshire: tower and garderobe turret.

42. Warkworth Castle, Northumberland: window flue in the great hall of the donjon.

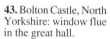

43. Bolton Castle, North Yorkshire: window flue in the great hall.

44. Bamburgh Castle, Northumberland: window flue in the kitchen of 1384–7.

45. Bolton Castle: squinch arch.

46. Raby Castle, Durham: squinch arch.

Bolton and Bamburgh (figures 42, 43 and 44). Another is the use of squinch arches to support the corner turrets at Bolton and a number of other castles around Durham (figures 45 and 46). Although the concepts are the same, the execution of the details is not necessarily identical, and all are capable of having been delegated to a subordinate by word of mouth. In such circumstances the master mason may have occupied a similar role to that of the patron in respect of design; instruction by word of mouth and, in some cases, reference to a mutually known model, might have been sufficient guidance for a suitably qualified deputy.

Glossary

Arcade: a series of arches carried on columns, either free-standing and load-bearing or blind and applied to wall surfaces as decoration.

Ashlar: blocks of stone worked to square edges and even faces, for laying in finely jointed horizontal courses.

Barbican: a fortified outwork protecting a gateway.

Bay: a vertical division of a building, defined by windows, buttresses, arcades or vaulting compartments.

Capital: the element at the head of a column, colonette or pilaster, usually decorated with mouldings or carvings.

Centring: a timber framework used to support arches and vaulting during construction and kept in position until the mortar has set.

Choir: the part of a church in which the service is sung, east of the nave and west of the presbytery. The term is sometimes applied in an architectural sense to the whole of the eastern arm of the building, but the choir itself often extends into the crossing and sometimes into the nave.

Cinquefoil: a five-lobed figure.

Cloister garth: the open quadrangle surrounded by the roofed or vaulted passages of the cloister.

Clunch: a soft limestone.

Coin: an early spelling of *quoin*.

Corbel: a stone projecting from the face of a wall to support a load.

Crossing: the area, often surmounted by a tower, where the nave, chancel and transepts of a cruciform-plan church intersect.

Dressed stone: finished stone, though not necessarily worked to as great a degree of precision as ashlar.

Freestone: any type of stone that can be worked freely, a quality that is often associated with fine-grained limestone or sandstone.

Hurdles: rectangular wooden frames plaited with *withies*; often used as scaffolding platforms in the Middle Ages.

Jamb: the side of an opening such as a window, doorway or fireplace.

Joggle: the break or rebate in the line of a joint between two stones, made to prevent slipping or sliding.

Mistery: a trade or craft involving specialist knowledge and skill on the part of the practitioner.

Moulding: a decoration on buildings comprising a shaped profile.

Perch: a measure of length, usually 16 feet 6 inches (5.03 metres), though perches of different lengths were used in the medieval period.

Pinnacle: a tall, narrow, usually conical termination, often used to crown buttresses and the angles of parapets.

Postern: a small gateway, sometimes to the rear of a building, but also a pedestrian entrance to the side of a carriage gateway.

Quatrefoil: a four-lobed figure.

Quoins: blocks of dressed stone used to form the corners between walls, often of greater size or more carefully formed than those that make up the walls.

Rib vaulting: vaulting based on a framework of stone arches (or ribs). The compartments between the ribs are infilled with *webbing*.

Rough walling: rubble walling.

Scarf joint: a technique used in joining together the ends of two lengths of timber.

Slaking: the process of adding water to quicklime to produce lime putty.

Squinch arch: an arch built diagonally across the right angle formed by two adjoining walls to support an upper structure.

Transept: a transverse element projecting from the side of a church, usually between the chancel and the nave, and roofed at right angles to the main axis.

Transitional: the period of transition between the Romanesque and Gothic styles of architecture, dating from *c*.1150 to *c*.1220.

Triforium: an arcaded wall passage or blind arcade above the main arcade and below the clerestory.

Voussoirs: wedge-shaped stones used to make up an arch.

Warrant: a written authority for receiving money or for obtaining goods or services.

Webbing: the infilled compartments of a rib vault.

Withies: strong, pliant branches, often willow, used in binding scaffolding together and in the construction of walls.

Further reading

General works

Andrews, F.B. *The Medieval Builders and Their Methods*. Dover Publications, 1999. A reprint of texts published in 1922 and 1928.

Coldstream, Nicola. *Medieval Craftsmen: Masons and Sculptors*. British Museum Press, 1991.

Erlande-Brandenburg, A. *The Cathedral Builders of the Middle Ages*. Translated by Rosemary Stonehewer. Thames & Hudson, 1995. First published in France in 1993.

Gimpel, J. *The Cathedral Builders*. Translated by Teresa Waugh. Pimlico, 1993. First published in France in 1980.

Harvey, J.H. *The Mediaeval Architect*. Wayland, 1972.

Knoop, Douglas, and Jones, G.P. *The Medieval Mason*. Manchester University Press, revised edition 1967.

Maude, Thomas. *Guided by a Stone Mason*. I. B. Tauris Publishers, 1997.

Shelby, Lon R. 'The Role of the Master Mason in Medieval English Building', *Speculum,* 39 (1964), 387–403.

Documentary evidence

Brown, R.A., Colvin, H.M., and Taylor, A.J. *The History of the King's Works. Volumes 1–2: The Middle Ages*. HMSO, 1963.

Colvin, H.M., and Hector, L.C. (editors). *Building Accounts of Henry III*. Oxford University Press, 1972.

Erskine, A. (editor). *The Accounts of the Fabric of Exeter Cathedral*. Devon and Cornwall Record Society, 24 (1981); 26 (1983).

Harvey, J.H. *English Mediaeval Architects*. Alan Sutton, revised edition 1983.

Salzman, L.F. *Building in England Down to 1540*. Oxford University Press, 1952; revised edition 1967; special edition for Sandpiper Books, 1997.

Design

Bony, J. 'The Stonework Planning of the First Durham Master' in *Medieval Architecture and Its Intellectual Context*, edited by Fernie and Crossley. Hambledon Press, 1990.

Fernie, E. 'The Ground Plan of Norwich Cathedral and the Square Root of Two', *Journal of the British Archaeological Association*, 129 (1976), 78–86.

Heslop, T.A. 'Orford Castle, Nostalgia and Sophisticated Living', *Architectural History*, 34 (1991), 35–58.

Hislop, M.J.B., 'Bolton Castle and the Practice of Architecture in the Middle Ages', *Journal of the British Archaeological Association*, 149 (1996), 10–22.

Construction methods

Butler, Lawrence. 'Masons' Marks in Castles: a Key to Building Practice', *Château Gaillard,* 18 (1998), 23–7.

Fitchen, J. *The Construction of Gothic Cathedrals.* Chicago University Press, 1961.

Hill, P.R. 'Stonework and the Archaeologist Including a Stonemason's View of Hadrian's Wall', *Archaeologia Aeliana,* fifth series 9 (1981), 1–22.

Parsons, David. *Stone: Quarrying and Building in England AD 43–1525.* Phillimore, in association with the Royal Archaeological Institute, 1990.

Phillips, Derek (RCHM). *Excavations at York Minster. Volume II: The Cathedral of Archbishop Thomas of Bayeux.* HMSO, 1985.

Rodwell, W. *The Archaeology of the English Church.* Batsford, 1981.

Identifying master masons

Dixon, P.W. 'Hillslap Tower, Masons and Regional Traditions', *History of the Berwickshire Naturalists Club,* 40 (1979), 128–41.

Fawcett, R. 'A Group of Churches by the Architect of Great Walsingham', *Norfolk Archaeology,* 37, 3 (1980), 277–94.

Fawcett, R. 'St Mary at Wiveton in Norfolk, and a Group of Churches Attributed to Its Mason', *Antiquaries Journal,* 62, part 1 (1982), 35–56.

Harvey, J.H. *Henry Yevele.* Batsford, 1944.

Hislop, M.J.B. 'John Lewyn of Durham: a North Country Mason of the Fourteenth Century', *Journal of the British Archaeological Association,* 151 (1998), 170–89.

Maddison, J.M. 'Master Masons of the Diocese of Lichfield: a Study in 14th Century Architecture at the Time of the Black Death', *Transactions of the Lancashire and Cheshire Antiquarian Society,* 85 (1988).

McLees, A. David. 'Henry Yevele: Disposer of the King's Works of Masonry', *Journal of the British Archaeological Association,* third series 36–7 (1973–4), 52–71.

Morris, R.K. 'Thomas of Witney at Exeter, Wells and Winchester', *Medieval Art and Architecture at Exeter,* British Archaeological Association Conference Transactions, 11 (1991), 57–84.

Petch, M.R. 'William de Malton Master Mason', *Yorkshire Archaeological Journal,* 53 (1981), 37–44.

Roberts, E. 'Moulding Analysis and Architectural Research: the Late Middle Ages', *Architectural History,* 20 (1977), 5–13.

Taylor, A.J. 'Master James of St George', *English Historical Review,* 65 (1950), 433–47.

Taylor, A.J. 'The Castle of St Georges d'Esperanche', *Antiquaries Journal,* 33 (1953), 33–47.

Index